THE VIENNA NOTES

Richard Nelson

I0139928

BROADWAY PLAY PUBLISHING INC
New York
www.broadwayplaypub.com
info@broadwayplaypub.com

THE VIENNA NOTES
© Copyright 1988 Richard Nelson

First published by B P P I in *Plays By Richard Nelson, Early Plays, Volume Two* in December 1998
This edition: December 2017

I S B N: 978-0-88145-718-6

Book design: Marie Donovan
Page make-up: Adobe InDesign
Typeface: Palatino

THE VIENNA NOTES was first presented in workshop at Guthrie II, directed by Bruce Siddons.

THE VIENNA NOTES was produced by Playwrights Horizons (André Bishop, Artistic Director; Robert Moss, Producing Director) on 18 January 1979. The cast and creative contributors were:

STUBBS .... Dan Desmond
RIVERS..Kate McGregor-Stewart
GEORGIA ....Marcell Rosenblatt
GUNTER .... Richard Bey

Director.. André Ernotte
Set designer.. Heidi Landesman
Costume designer....................................William Ivey Long
Lighting designer .... Paul Gallo
Special effects ....Jack Stewart
Sound designer.. David Rapkin

CHARACTERS & SETTING

Stubbs, *a politician*
Rivers, *his secretary*
Georgia
Gunter, *a porter*

*An intimate hotel in Vienna and a country house outside
Vienna.*

Scene One

(Setting: Vienna. The sitting room of a suite in an old and intimate hotel.)

(Upstage center, a handsome antique writing desk faces the audience.)

(Left, a red velvet divan, laced with fringe, a potted fern, and two small tables, one with a lamp, the other with a black telephone.)

(Door to the hallway, right.)

(Stage dark. Lights fade up.)

(Pause)

(The door is opened. GEORGIA, STUBBS, RIVERS, and finally GUNTER enter. GEORGIA [early thirties] is well and fashionably dressed. [She is the Chairwoman of the Lecture Committee for the Vienna Americans' Club.] STUBBS [fifties] wears a nicely fitting overcoat and a Russian-style fur hat. [He is a U S Senator.] RIVERS [late forties] wears a cloth coat, not very stylish. [She is STUBBS' secretary.] GUNTER is the porter and he carries in the suitcases.)

GEORGIA: *(Entering)* Well? What did I tell you? Just what did I tell you? Was I right? Or was I right?

(GEORGIA looks for a reaction but gets none. STUBBS has begun to take off his coat, loosen his tie, etc, all the while taking in the room. RIVERS just stands for the moment and looks around.)

GEORGIA: It's everything I said it was, isn't it? *(She looks for a reaction, but gets none.)* And you can't believe your eyes, can you? *(No response)* Vienna! City of mystery. City of ambiance. City of Mozart. City with that Old World charm. That musty charm. You can just breathe it. Breathe it!

RIVERS: *(Who wasn't listening)* What?

GEORGIA: Breathe!

(RIVERS breathes.)

GEORGIA: Vienna! City of intrigue. City of cafes. City of wine. Of singing. Of glittering chandeliers. And it's all right here before us. All of it. The best part. You can just see it all right here. And feel it. Go 'head! *(No response; short pause)* And that lace. Just look at that lace. And that velvet. Incredible. And look at the craftsmanship in that desk. Do you believe that? Do you believe that! *(Short pause; no reaction)* Well, I can't. I've lived here almost two years and I still can't. I mean, you don't find three hundred-year-old rooms like this in America, unless they're carved into the side of a cliff. Am I right? Or am I right?

RIVERS: *(Taking off her coat; not really paying attention)* You're right.

GEORGIA: I knew you'd say that. I just knew it. Because you know why? Because that's exactly how I felt. I felt the same way. When Winslow and I arrived here. *(Smiles to herself; almost laughs)* Boy, do I remember that.

(As GEORGIA continues talking, she opens her purse and looks for a handkerchief. But before she finds one, she has to first take out a few items—a compact, an address book, and a snub-nosed revolver. RIVERS notices but is not terribly surprised.)

GEORGIA: Brother. Did you know I was disappointed at first? It's true. I was. My first glance. We got off the plane and God only knows what I was expecting to find. But it certainly wasn't just another airport. An ordinary old airport. Winslow says my face dropped a good foot. And I'll bet it did. 'Cause all I was thinking, see, was: Georgia, girl, you could be anywhere. This is just an airport. I thought that. Admittedly, the jet lag didn't help. But I. I'll admit it. On first glance I was terribly disappointed. Isn't that crazy? *(She looks around and realizes no one is listening.)* Gunter, take the bags into the bedrooms.

STUBBS: *(Who has been looking over some scraps of paper he had in his pants pocket; without looking up:)* Not the brown one. That oughta stay out here.

(GUNTER leaves the brown bag and exits left with the others.)

(Pause)

(GEORGIA looks around, waiting for someone to say something.)

GEORGIA: *(Finally)* And then we took a taxi. A Mercedes. At least that's a difference, I told myself. But the ride, itself. Well, it wasn't much. Was it? It wasn't anything really. Anything to write home about, that is. I mean, the same city sounds, you know. The same sort of smells, you know. The same chuckholes you could find anywhere. Maybe there was a bit more police around. You know, checking cars. That kind of thing. But that isn't something you'd jump for joy about, right? *(Short pause. No reaction)* So I guess you could say—are you with me?

(STUBBS and RIVERS have opened the brown bag and are rummaging through it, taking out notebooks, files, thumbing through these, sorting them out and piling some on the desk.)

GEORGIA: So I guess you could say. That by the time we pulled up in front of the hotel. As a matter of fact this same hotel. *(No reaction)* You could say, I wanted to go home. I was nearly in tears. I'd expected something mysterious. Something, you know, Viennese. But all I'd got was, well, you know. And then we got into the lift. And I remember feeling so tired and so resentful, but thinking in utter disbelief, mind you, that Winslow— and that meant me too—that Winslow had a contract to stay put here for three years. Three whole years! Do you believe that? *(No reaction, feeling more and more self-conscious)* And so on that note. I remember this so well. Listen. We walked into our room. It wasn't this room. But the effect is the same. And I saw the antiques. And my mouth opened. And I saw the fringe on the lamps. And I got a lump in my throat. I felt the velvet. And it was velvet. And all of a sudden. I found myself shaking. I was shaking. I was! I found myself almost spellbound. I had to pinch myself. Pinch, I said! Pinch! And I turned to Winslow. And tears began to roll down my cheeks. I stretched out my arms. This is wonderful, I wanted to say. But the words wouldn't come out. But I guess he knew what I was thinking. Because he smiled. And I remember laughing. Just laughing, you know, as the tears, they just streamed down my face.

(STUBBS has unplugged the lamp on the table and has taken it over to the desk.)

STUBBS: *(To RIVERS)* You see a socket?

RIVERS: *(Still going through the bag)* There's gotta be one somewhere around the desk, Stubbs.

(Pause)

(GEORGIA, now very self-conscious, very confused, tries to get a hold of herself. She goes to RIVERS and taps her on the shoulder. RIVERS looks up.)

GEORGIA: So you like it? The room, I mean.

RIVERS: *(Looks around)* It's nice. *(Returns to the bag)*

GEORGIA: You mean that?

STUBBS: I can't find one.

RIVERS: Just a sec. I'll look.

(RIVERS goes to the desk, leaving GEORGIA alone.)

GEORGIA: I knew you would. I knew you'd like it. So I guess all the trouble I went through was worth it, right? *(No response)* With my club, I mean. In talking it out. In coming to an agreement. There's a lot that had to be taken into account. It wasn't all that easy. Believe me. A lot. In choosing a hotel for a guest speaker. Especially for a Senator. Especially for a Senator who'd been a whisker away, right, from being a President. There's a whole lot. Isn't there?

RIVERS: Here's a socket that cord would reach.

(STUBBS unravels the cord, plugs it in.)

GEORGIA: But do you know what finally made us decide? On this hotel? It was something *I* said. Do you want to hear?

(RIVERS returns to the bar.)

GEORGIA: Do you really? I said. Listen to this. I said, if he is going to visit Vienna. If Senator Stubbs is going to be our guest in Vienna. Then, damn it, he should visit Vienna. Do you see what I meant?

(No response: STUBBS at the desk, looking through papers)

GEORGIA: You do? *(No response)* Well, was I right? *(No response)* Or was I right? *(No response. She is upset, though making a great effort to control herself.)*

STUBBS: *(Without looking up)* I got a few notes in my coat, Rivers.

RIVERS: I'll get 'em. *(She does.)*

(Pause)

(GEORGIA *doesn't know what to do.* GUNTER, *who returned a few moments ago, has been standing left, waiting.*)

GUNTER: *(To* GEORGIA*)* Now?

GEORGIA: *(Almost yells:)* What?! Oh, right. I'm sorry. I nearly forgot. Sure, Gunter. Go ahead and tell your story. God knows, maybe they'll be interested in that.

(GEORGIA *sits on the divan:* GUNTER *moves center, clears his throat. Every so often,* STUBBS *and* RIVERS *pick up their heads for a second and listen to* GUNTER, *but for most of the time they ignore him and continue what they've been doing.*)

GUNTER: It was a winter's evening, one hundred and twenty years ago tonight. The crowd lining Kartnerstrasse was three deep as Franz Josef's white carriage rattled along. Peasants in red scarves cheered. The gypsies rang bells. Others waved and bowed. The wheels of the carriage made a clapping sound over the cobble stone. And the breath of the horses created small clouds in the air.

At the Opera House, the carriage door was opened by an attendant dressed in gold. He held his hat and bowed. All in one movement. And the Emperor walked out. "Oh!" gasped the crowd. Then absolute silence, except for the scraping noise of Franz Josef's sword against the Opera steps. The mammoth wooden doors opened seemingly by themselves, and the Emperor slightly tilted his head to acknowledge the crowd. Which then went wild.

Once inside, the Emperor took his royal box. The opera that evening was *Faust.* Ambassadors stood and raised their plumed hats to the box. Women hid their faces, though not their eyes. The orchestra stood and saluted the salute they had practiced earlier that day. And then the overture began. And the music sounded heavenly.

While Faust was singing his doubts, Franz Josef
scanned the audience with a pair of opera glasses.
They had been a gift from the Dutch Ambassador. In
return, the Emperor had given Holland a very fine
harpsichordist. Everyone was satisfied. The conductor
was nervous, and drops of perspiration formed like
beads on the top of his bald head. And Faust sang his
heart out.

Suddenly, a woman, not in a box, but in the loge,
caught the Emperor's eye. He twitched. He felt his
stomach tighten. He examined her closely through
the glasses. He could not take his eyes off her. Franz
Josef consulted with his ministers. But no one knew
her name. Ushers went scurrying to other boxes. The
French Ambassador thought she might be French. The
Opera House was filled with whispers. Even the singer
playing Mephistopheles glanced her way. Finally, the
curtain for the interval came down.

Attendants rushed to the woman's seat. But only
to find her gone. Hallways were quickly searched.
Carriages which lined the streets were examined.
Franz Josef was beside himself. "Find her!" he yelled.
And ministers hid behind each other. Then, just as the
Emperor was about to give up hope, a small young
man brought to him a white glove. It had been left
under her seat, he said. And the Emperor handed the
man a coin. Franz Josef held the glove loose in his
hand. He tried to smell it. He held it up to the light. He
played with it as if it were alive. Then. A card fell out.
Franz Josef screamed at his ministers to stand back.
There was an address on the card.

Franz Josef gave his driver the address. The horses
were whipped. The carriage lurched back. A beggar
was nearly run over. "Faster!" shouted the Emperor.
"Faster!" he continued to shout, until the driver had
finally replied, "We're here."

And so Franz Josef found himself standing before this very hotel. My great great grandfather almost fainted as he bowed. The Emperor took two stairs at once. He appeared almost to fly. His heart obviously was racing. He found the door without much trouble. He checked the number with that on the card a third, and then a fourth time. It matched. It matched. He smelled the glove which he still held loose in his hand. And then. Then he pounded. He pounded harder. And the door creaked as it opened. And Franz Josef, Emperor of the Austrian- Hungarian Empire, was heard to sigh. And the door swiftly closed behind him. *(Short pause)* Three hours later, the Emperor left this hotel.

(Pause)

(GUNTER *exits right.)*

(GEORGIA *waits for a reaction.)*

GEORGIA: *(Finally:)* Well? *(No response)* Isn't that incredible? Can you believe that? Doesn't it just make your skin crawl? *(No response)* See, it was this hotel. This same hotel. Right here. That happened right here!! *(No response; she explodes.)* GOD DAMN IT! HERE!! HERE!! WILL YOU PAY ATTENTION!! HE DOESN'T TELL THAT TO EVERYONE!!! THAT WAS SPECIAL!! THAT WAS SUPPOSED TO BE A TREAT!!! I PAID HIM TWENTY BUCKS TO DO THAT!!! LISTEN!!! LISTEN!!!

(RIVERS *looks up.* STUBBS *has "snuck" a glance but keeps writing in a notebook.* GEORGIA *tries to calm herself, to put on a "better face".)*

GEORGIA: I'm sorry. I don't know what got into me. Did I tell you how much I've looked forward to this? I have. Really. Meeting you? Greeting you? I must have imagined, you know. In the mirror. Before falling asleep. I must have imagined a thousand times what I'd say to you. To make you comfortable. To get you to enjoy yourself. Give you a good time. But I never really imagined. Not this. *(Short pause; erupts again)* LOOK! I'VE GONE TO A FUCKING LOT OF TROUBLE FOR YOU!!

(STUBBS and RIVERS watch; short pause; then nearly out of control:)

GEORGIA: Look. I may be a nobody. Okay. Georgia nobody. Granted. Fine. I will buy that. But it seems to me. It just seems to me. Am I wrong? Tell me if I'm wrong. But it just seems to me that that don't mean you couldn't have. You couldn't have. Well, does it? DOES IT!! *(No response)* DOES IT!!!! Okay, Jesus, maybe I'm not the smartest. Maybe I'm no big shot. But you could have. DAMN IT, YES YOU COULD HAVE PRETENDED!!! *(Pause. She goes to the door, opens it, looks back, no response. She exits, slamming the door.)*

RIVERS: We'll see you tonight then? Nine-thirty, wasn't it? *(She returns to her work.)*

GEORGIA: *(Quickly reentering; hopeful:)* What? What did you say? *(No response)* Were you talking to me? *(No response. She turns slowly, defeated, and exits, closing the door gently this time.)*

(Pause)

(STUBBS remains staring at the door, obviously thinking.)

RIVERS: *(Notices he isn't working)* What's the matter, Stubbs?

STUBBS: Oh, boy.

RIVERS: Hey, I thought you couldn't wait to knock off this entry? Come on. *(Short pause)* What's wrong with you? You said you couldn't concentrate on the plane so as soon as we could get set. Well, we're just about set. Stubbs, we're set.

(Finally notices he's thinking, has that look which she has seen so many times before)

RIVERS: Oh. I get you. I think I'm with you. But when the hell did that happen? When did you get another one? About the girl? Is it about the girl?

STUBBS: Maybe. We'll just have to see, won't we? See if it plays.

RIVERS: Then you want me to get ready to write?

STUBBS: What? Yeh. That's a good idea. Get yourself ready. 'Cause this kinda thing you gotta get while it's hot.'Cause it's gonna be all detail. All in tiny bits. Now sit on the couch and give me some room for this. Some breathing space. *(Still staring)* Okay. Okay. It might just be nice. You got a notebook?

RIVERS: I had to get a new one. The last was about full.

STUBBS: So what's the number?

RIVERS: The last was eighty-three.

STUBBS: *(Still staring)* So then it's notebook number eighty four. Put it down.

(RIVERS writes.)

STUBBS: "The Memoirs of Henry Stubbs, United States Senator." Put in the date.

RIVERS: *(Writes)* Done.

STUBBS: *(Still staring)* Good. Very good.

(Suddenly STUBBS breaks his stare and begins getting into what he says; RIVERS writes.)

STUBBS: My hotel suite. Vienna. I had just flown in from the U S. Still with that taste. That stale airplane taste in my mouth. Uncomfortable. With aching legs. Feeling tired. Weak. Not quite all there. Not quite solid. The jet-sound still inside me. Still echoing. Drumming. Pulsing. So, feeling first, that I had better get down to

work. And second, that I wanted to stretch out. Relax.
Maybe a hot bath would be nice.
So as I walked in. Off went the coat. The tie was
loosened. The file case unpacked. A place of work
set up. To get cracking. To get to the point where
I wouldn't feel guilty about stretching out. And
unwinding. And taking it slow and easy. So all this
while I looked around. Took things in. Not bad, I
thought. This suite. Got a certain. *Je ne sais quoi.* A
feeling to it. A certain charm. That I like. That pleased
me.
So all this while my hostess. From the Americans'
Club. Where I'm to deliver a lecture tonight. *(Quickly
turns to* RIVERS, *snaps his fingers)* Name!

RIVERS: *(Writing)* Georgia.

STUBBS: *(Continuing)* By the name of Georgia. So all
this while I heard her talk. About this and that. About
Vienna this. Mozart that. Even something about
Mercedes. I heard only fragments as they cracked
my concentration. I heard only the strain. The tone
of the voice. And this, for an instant, concerned me.
Something odd. Something out of whack. It nicked me.
I rubbed my eyes. I wondered, what kind of talk is…?
But before I could finish the thought, the voice became
silent. Still. And the porter… *(Turns to* RIVERS) The
porter?

*(*RIVERS *nods.)*

STUBBS: He took over for a while.
So there was a calm. In retrospect, I would probably
say, a calm before the storm. But then, there was just
a calm, in which I turned back to my work. Back to
the desk. Back to my fingers, which I watched move
silently across the piece of paper. Back to urging
myself. Telling myself, concentrate. Concentrate. And
"hot bath".

But soon. How long? I'd lost touch. Lost a feel for the
time. Like maybe a rash one first feels before it turns
red. Just a hint. Just an itch. I felt this sudden. This
growing sensation. Tension. Around me. In the room.
It seemed to be pressing up against me. Nudging me.
It seemed to have somehow changed the complexion.
Of the air. The atmosphere here. Blurring it. Confusing
it. Just a general fuzzy sensation that something was
about to. On the very verge of. What is going...?
But before I could even get the words into my brain.
The sensation, it was past that point. Past the point
of dealing with. Way the hell past. Because this
woman's voice. It was back. Like gangbusters. This
Georgia. I was hearing her now shout: "GOD DAMN
IT! GOD DAMN IT!" So what I'd felt to be growing
like an itch, was now, well now it was building. It
was crescendoing. Her words, gaining speed. Faster.
What is she...? FASTER! Too god damn fast. Getting
run together. Sounding to my ears more like emotions
now. More like tiny little screams: "ATTENTION!!"
"SPECIAL!!" "FUCKING TROUBLE!!"
I listened. I craned my ears. If that's possible. If that
is feasible. But no sense. Found nonsense. So I'm just
telling myself, these things; these annoyances. These
obnoxious annoyances. They happen. They can't be.
No help. They just come with the position. Of being
powerful. Of being well known. So what is the use.
What's the. Just gotta tolerate it, that's all. Just gotta
live with this, sort of. TOLERATE!! I scream at myself.
And I jam my finger into the paper, trying to doodle
a circle. What can I do? So I draw a crowd. So people
stare at me. So I'm just shown to my hotel suite
and a woman. This woman, she is screaming: "I'M
NOBODY!!" SO WHAT THE HELL CAN I DO?!!!
THAT'S YOUR PROBLEM!! I want to scream. I want to
shove my face at her and scream.

And then. As I am shaking my head and thinking, not
much more. There's not much more of this I can take.
Well, she is just hitting her stride. What had come
before. What had come out before sounding like a last-
breath effort. Well now, now, it sounds like an offhand
comment compared to. With this. "THAT DOES IT!!!"
I'm thinking the same thing. "THAT DOES IT!!" Then:
"DAMN IT!!" Then: "YOU COULD HAVE!" I'm biting
my lip. BITE! Then: "YOU COULD HAVE!!!" I'm
rubbing my face. I'm thinking: hold back. Hold back.
Then, finally: "YOU COULD HAVE PRETENDED!!!!"
(Short pause)
Then calm. A couple of heart beats. What next? I
loosen my grip and drop my pen. Like a pin dropped.
That quiet. Then. BANG!! And I jump as the door was
slammed shut. And I'm thinking. Boy, am I thinking:
"hot bath. Hot bath. Hot bath."

(Short pause. RIVERS *writes.* STUBBS, *out of breath, though
suddenly now businesslike, out of the story)*

STUBBS: Okay. That's it. Not bad. Not half bad. Maybe a
little rough in spots. But what the hell. We can fix that.
(To RIVERS*)* Mark my thoughts for italics.

RIVERS: Right.

STUBBS: Maybe a bit slow here and there. Can't tell yet.
It felt okay. Not wonderful. But okay. *(To* RIVERS*)* You
done?

RIVERS: *(Writing)* Just about.

STUBBS: Well, check *her* words. Make sure you have 'em
all in quotes. I don't want any confusion 'bout who the
hell said what.

RIVERS: I always check, Stubbs.

STUBBS: The opening. Definitely. The opening was
sluggish. I could feel that. I remember feeling just that.
Loose. Very loose. "I did this. I did that." I mean, Jesus,

if people are really gonna get this into. I mean, go through it themselves. If they're gonna be empathizing themselves blue. If they're really gonna get the picture of the kind of stuff I go through. Or, depending. Depending on when the hell they read this, of the kind of stuff I went through in my life. Then, Christ. Playing loose. Playing loose, especially early. That won't do. You gotta let `em in. And let 'em in fast.

RIVERS: Done.

STUBBS: What? Oh great. Let me see that. Who knows, maybe I'm wrong. Maybe I'm wrong and it just seemed loose at the time.

(STUBBS *looks over the notebook. The door opens.* GEORGIA *enters with great hesitation.*)

GEORGIA: I. I got halfway home. And I. Well I suddenly remembered that I'd forgot to tell you.

(RIVERS *looks at her;* STUBBS *ignores or doesn't really hear her.*)

GEORGIA: You won't say no, will you? It's not that far. Just a few kilometers. *(Short pause)* Winslow's home getting ready. *(Short pause)* If you're worried about getting back. If that's it. Well, you shouldn't. That shouldn't be a problem. *(Short pause)* You really won't say no, will you? *(Short pause)* But if you'd rather not.... It you have other plans. *(Short pause)* If you're tired. *(Short pause)* If you want to be alone. *(Short pause)* If you would really rather not.

RIVERS: Rather not what, Georgia?

GEORGIA: Uh. Come to *my* house. For dinner.

RIVERS: Well, Stubbs?

STUBBS: *(Looking at the notebook. Suddenly:)* GOD DAMN IT!!!

(Looks up, notices both RIVERS *and* GEORGIA *are looking at him)*

STUBBS: It is sluggish. *(Short pause)* Well, what? I wasn't listening.

(Blackout)

Scene Two

(Setting: GEORGIA *and Winslow's rented converted farmhouse. The living room.)*

(Upstage left and angled center—door, paned windows with drapes on either side of the door. This on a platform, so there is a step down to the living room proper.)

(Center: sofa, table with vase, wooden bench, coffee table, telephone, oriental rug, etc.)

(Stage dark. Lights up)

(Door opens. GEORGIA, RIVERS, *and then* STUBBS *enter.* RIVERS *writes in her notebook.* GEORGIA *listens fascinated.)*

STUBBS: *(Entering; he is "into" his story, feeling almost everything he says.)* And the hum. Drone. Soothed me. Almost massaged. For moments, I felt myself almost encased by the sound. Like in a bubble. Like in a cell. And the lights, they jarred. First, the street lamps. While still driving through the city. Then the oncoming cars. Their lights flickered quickly across my face. It felt almost like I was blinking.

GEORGIA: *(Taking off her coat; quietly, to* RIVERS:*)* He said, this is for his memoirs?

RIVERS: *(Writing)* Sh-sh.

GEORGIA: I'm sorry.

STUBBS: *(Continuing)* So I closed my eyes. An effort. The window had been rolled down. I stuck my face.

Almost shoved it. Into the rush of night air. At first, the urge. The impulse to hold my hair. Keep it out of my eyes. But eventually. Finally. I let it blow. There was conversation in the front seat. That much I knew. But just "conversation". Because the wind. The drone. All combined. It sounded like a foreign language.

GEORGIA: This is exciting. (*Loud whisper*) Winslow! Come and hear this!

STUBBS: A reach for a cigarette. The explosion of the match. The glow. I felt down the side of the door. Where's the ashtray? Georgia had to tell me where it was. I can find it, I thought. I CAN FIND IT!!!

GEORGIA: (*To* RIVERS; *trying to be quiet*) He's gonna use that? What *I* said?

STUBBS: I felt old. My hand on the leather seat. Never that smooth. My skin was never that smooth. I looked around me. The blue dashboard light. The red glow. The oncoming cars. A landscape. A landscape of dreams.

GEORGIA: Could you hold it a minute. Just until I got Winslow. You couldn't imagine what a thrill he'd get. (*She exits left.*)

STUBBS: And then I saw myself. Don't be sentimental, I wanted to say. Don't be indulgent. But I saw myself like this. Like here. Other cars. In other back seats. Other cities. Countries. Drivers. All blurred. All stuck together. I wanted to reach into my brain and pull them apart. I saw a Spaniard with medals pinned to his chest. The two of us. Back seat. But where? Then I saw papers. Briefs for 'eyes only'. Piled across my lap. My head buried. My head hidden. Now I'm alone. And now police cars both front and back. Where is... And now there. THERE! DID YOU FEEL THAT?!! That was the thump as we drove across a median. Because this is urgent. See, this. Essential. This. What is this?

GEORGIA: *(Off)* Winslow!

STUBBS: And now my arms. Outstretched. The top down. And a beauty queen both left and. And right. And we're smiling. We're. This a parade of. Marking what? For what…? But the sunshine I can definitely feel the… But now it's blurred. Now it is in the middle of the. It's pitch. It's. I can't see a thing. Just my driver. We're waiting for. This, an Army airstrip. We're waiting for an important. For some. And he and I. We're ol' buddies. We are. We're shooting the bull. Talking good ol'. Football. And smoking. We were smoking. We were.

GEORGIA: *(Off)* Winslow!

STUBBS: Then I coughed. As I rubbed out my cigarette. And I could feel the veins. The forehead veins. Pulse blood. Straining. Knew my face, now beet. Now bright red. And my chest. My chest, it aches. And I rubbed at my brain. Almost. Wanted to. Nearly kneaded it. Until I could finally. Just close my eyes. Shut them. Without it hurting.

GEORGIA: *(Entering; concerned)* I even looked on the porch.

(She exits right, to check out the bedrooms)

STUBBS: *(After a brief pause)* And when I finally woke. Because the light overhead had come on. Because Rivers' voice, I heard it now, was outside the car. She's out there tapping on the window and saying. What's she saying. That I'm old? That I'm feeble? That I get things sometimes mixed up? Is she saying where we…? What city? What country? What's she telling me? What am I supposed to know that she's telling me! Speak up! Rivers, speak up! WHAT!! WHAT!! TELL ME!! TELL ME!! I DON'T KNOW WHERE I AM!!! *(Pause)* But Rivers. When I finally can make it. Understand. All she is saying. She's just saying, "We're here." *(Short pause. He suddenly breaks out of the story.)* That's it. What did you do with my cigarettes?

RIVERS: *(Writing)* You had 'em in the car, Stubbs. You want me to check?

STUBBS: You got that down?

RIVERS: *(Writing)* I will in a minute.

STUBBS: Then you finish. I'll go hunt them up.

GEORGIA: *(Off)* Winslow!

(STUBBS opens the door, then turns back to RIVERS.)

STUBBS: What did you think? It wasn't what you'd call loud. Not in fucking neon. But the old guy just remembering. There's a built-in thing in that. The situation itself, I would think, oughta be enough to grab 'em and hold them in. Don't you?

RIVERS: *(Writing; sincerely:)* It was nice, Stubbs. Really. Just real nice.

STUBBS: Good. You know, it was just so easy, you begin to get doubts.

RIVERS: Well, you shouldn't.

STUBBS: Thanks. *(Turns to exit, stops)* Who the hell is that?

RIVERS: *(Writing)* Somebody out there?

GEORGIA: Winslow! *(Off)*

RIVERS: *(Writing)* Must be her Winslow. *(Calling:)* He's outside!!

STUBBS: *(Looking out)* Boy, what a fucked-up place this is. I heard it was bad, but shit. Look at that, Rivers. You gotta carry a gun just to go outside your own house. That's somethin'.

RIVERS: *(Writing)* He's got a gun?

STUBBS: Which one is Winslow?

RIVERS: *(Stops writing, looks up)* Which *one*?

STUBBS: Yeh, there's at least… And what the hell do they have on their faces?

(Suddenly, off, GEORGIA screams at the top of her lungs.)

(RIVERS sets the notebook down.)

STUBBS: What is wrong with her? *(Returns to looking out the door)* It looks like… They're in a shadow. I'll be able to tell when they get closer.

(RIVERS looks toward where GEORGIA screamed from then back at STUBBS—something frightening begins to dawn on her.)

RIVERS: *(Forced calm)* Stubbs. Close the door.

STUBBS: Huh?

RIVERS: Just close it.

(STUBBS, confused, does so.)

RIVERS: *(Screams:)* NOW BOLT IT!!

STUBBS: What are you talking about?

(GEORGIA enters, in shock, blood stains on her hands and dress.)

RIVERS: *(Seeing her)* Oh, my God! OH NO!! NO!!!!

GEORGIA: *(Screams:)* THEY KILLED HIM!!!!!

RIVERS: Please, Stubbs. PLEASE BOLT THE FUCKING DOOR!!

(Very confused, STUBBS bolts the door and moves in front of the window.)

RIVERS: A gun. where's a gun? A GUN!! Think. Think. Okay. That's right. I saw one in her purse. Now where's her purse? *(Sees STUBBS at the window)* Stubbs, get away from the window.

(He doesn't move.)

RIVERS: Where's the purse? *(To* GEORGIA*)* WHERE'S YOUR GOD DAMN PURSE!!!

*(*GEORGIA *moves her hand.)*

RIVERS: Over there? Over where? I don't see it. Stubbs, do you see it? WHERE OVER THERE!!!

STUBBS: *(Confused, but calm)* It's on the couch. You want me to get it for you?

RIVERS: *(Seeing that* STUBBS *has not moved)* I WANT YOU TO GET DOWN!!!

STUBBS: Okay. *(Starts to stoop)*

RIVERS: DOWN!!!!!

*(*STUBBS *ducks down.)*

(Gun shot off, the window over STUBBS *shatters.)*

(He freezes.)

*(*GEORGIA *screams.)*

*(*RIVERS *has found the revolver, runs to the window, ducking down, raises the gun over her head.)*

RIVERS: *(Running to the windows)* DON'T COME ANY CLOSER!! DON'T COME ANY CLOSER!! *(She shoots four times:)* STOP! STOP! STOP! STOP!!!! *(Then she freezes, out of breath.)*

(Pause)

STUBBS: *(Picks up his head. peaks out the window)* They're gone. Or at least they're out of sight. *(He closes the curtain: to* RIVERS*)* They had ski masks on, didn't they?

GEORGIA: *(Screams:)* WINSLOW!!!!!!!!!!

(Everyone is still.)

(Long pause)

(Slowly, very slowly, STUBBS *and* RIVERS *relax, breathe easier. They get themselves together.* GEORGIA, *in shock, does not move.)*

STUBBS: *(Brushing himself off)* Not bad. Not bad at all. *(Short pause)* But not perfect. *(Short pause)* I know what could have been a lot better.

RIVERS: What do you mean, Stubbs?

STUBBS: What do I mean? I mean her. *(Nods toward* GEORGIA.*)*

*(*RIVERS *is confused.)*

STUBBS: I mean when we've got a situation thrown at us like we had here. Just had thrown at us. Well...her just coming in here and screaming her lungs out. Well, that doesn't add much, does it?

RIVERS: I'm still not following, Stubbs.

*(*GEORGIA *watches with growing disbelief.)*

STUBBS: Well, what I'm suggesting is, is that this could have been, well, what it almost was. And that is one of the most interesting. Most exciting. Most dramatic moments of my life. See, it *could have* been. But it wasn't.
Now that doesn't mean it wasn't any good. 'Cause it was. That's obvious. But great? No. No way. 'Cause, see, you don't do great by coming in here and screaming your lungs out. That could work, sure. But it'll work like the shockeroo that it is. Like the stick in the spokes. Like the tack on the chair that it is. Call it what you want. But whatever you call it, it's gonna come out meaning "slick". Meaning "easy". And meaning "cheap". You see what I'm saying now?

RIVERS: Yeh. I think so.

STUBBS: 'Cause, Jesus, where is the build there? In screaming like that. Where's the subtlety? God only knows. I mean, if you're gonna do it right, you gotta pluck it for all that it's worth. Like we did. Like you running around. Like you getting this. Getting that. Like me. "It's all slowly dawning on me." That kind of

stuff. That subtle stuff. But screaming? Doing shit but
screaming your lungs out? Tell me, where's the build
in that?

RIVERS: Yeh. I see what you mean. But what do you
think she should have done?

STUBBS: What do I think? Shit. There's a thousand.
There are possibilities. By the. There are millions. You
really want to know?

(RIVERS *nods.*)

STUBBS: Well. Let me think. She could have. Maybe.
Like maybe, she could have come in. You know,
without saying anything. No words. Nothing. But
maybe holding something. Like. *(Sees the phone book)*
Like a book. *(Picks up the phone book)* Okay? Like a
book. So she's holding a book. And. I haven't really
thought this out. And, she suddenly drops it. *(He drops
the book)* And she doesn't pick it up. Doesn't even look
down. Like she didn't even know she did anything. So
that's odd. That's peculiar. It's obvious something is
up, but nothing's been given away. Okay?

RIVERS: Okay.

STUBBS: And then. Maybe she plays with that bracelet.
Fasten it. Unfasten it. Her fingers tense. That's how
you notice they're shaking. First the bracelet, then
the tenseness. Sense of her holding back something.
Repressed. Ready to explode. But you don't really
know that yet. Just her nervousness, right?

RIVERS: Right.

STUBBS: Then. How about tears down her face. But
no sound. No crying. Just the tears. That's very
powerful. Very upsetting. And now a comment. She's
saying something. One thing. Something off the wall.
Something that is definitely gonna register, gonna click

a little "uh-oh" in the brain. A little, "What is going on here?" Something like...

RIVERS: "I keep seeing my father's face"?

STUBBS: What? Yeh. That's not bad. And her face blank. No expression whatever. And then she starts to take a step forward. One step. And as if just that little movement brought her back to. Back to her situation. Her hands quickly cover her face. She bends down, trying to remain tough. Remain self-possessed. But can't. Just can't. And then. At that time. Now she can explode. Now. Damn it now, she can scream her lungs out.

RIVERS: Yeh. That's pretty good.

STUBBS: So what do we have. (*He plays* "GEORGIA". *He drops the book*) The book.

RIVERS: (*Nodding*) The book. Yes.

STUBBS: I don't look down. (*He fiddles with his "bracelet". His hands are shaking.*) No expression on my face.

RIVERS: Right.

STUBBS: "1 keep seeing my father's face."

RIVERS: Good.

STUBBS: And tears. And... (*He starts to take a step. Covers his face, lowers his head slowly and suddenly screams*) Something like that. It *could have* been just great. (*Shakes his head*) You sure you don't have my cigarettes in your purse?

GEORGIA: (*Screams:*) WINSLOW!!!!!

STUBBS: See? See? That's just the kind of thing I've been talking about.

(*Blackout*)

Scene Three

(Setting: The same)

(Stage dark. Lights fade up.)

(RIVERS, *on the couch, holds her notebook.* STUBBS, *near her, standing and thinking.*)

(Pause)

STUBBS: *(To himself)* Okay. Maybe. Then: door. Then: duck. Then: bang. Then: okay. Right.

RIVERS: You ready?

STUBBS: Just a sec. I'm running it over. Then: yeh. And I'm feeling? Right. Uh-huh. I won't be long.

(GEORGIA *enters right. She carries a rifle, an automatic revolver, and an ammunition belt. She is still quite "dazed".)*

GEORGIA: *(Entering)* I found these in a closet. *(Holds them up; to* STUBBS*)* Which do you want? The pistol or the rifle?

(RIVERS *puts a finger to her lips, to "sh-sh"* GEORGIA*.)*

(Short pause)

GEORGIA: There's also this ammunition belt.

RIVERS: Georgia, not now.

(GEORGIA *just looks around, doesn't know what to do.)*

(STUBBS, *thinking, sighs.)*

GEORGIA: I'll give you the rifle. *(She sets the rifle and belt on the bench and sits.)*

STUBBS: *(Snaps his fingers)* Okay, Rivers. I think I'm set. So what the hell. Let's give it a go.

RIVERS: *(Set to write)* I'm right with you, Stubbs.

STUBBS: Right. Now just stay with me. *("Envisions" the scenes)* Farmhouse. Country. Outside Vienna. somewhere. God knows where. I didn't. I'm sure

I didn't. I'd just completed an entry. Not bad. Not
half bad. Nothing loud. Nothing in neon. And I was
thinking, that was easy. That was maybe too easy. So
doubts. So concerns. So I was going back over it and
thinking and reaching for a cigarette. But the pack's in
the car. Rivers tells me. So I was halfway out the door,
still fretting, when: who the hell is that? I said, who the
hell? Somebody's out there. Oh that must be, Rivers
said. Her. Her husband. Okay. So my mind, it moves
back a moment. Back a beat. Back to. To maybe it was
too god damn easy.
So then. Coming slowly into focus. A gun. Not a whole
gun. But the light on the porch reflected itself, say, as
a speck on the barrel of the gun. And that appeared to
bounce. The speck, that is. As the gun was moved. Boy
oh boy, I said. You gotta carry guns in this place. And
then. Suddenly, there are three. Not just guns, but men.
But not really men. But noses. Their faces, see, were
dark. Black. But their noses? Why? They were white.
Maybe they, I'm thinking. Maybe wearing what?
Mufflers? Beards? I even thought, maybe a native
costume. I did. How ridiculous. Do you believe that?
See how the mind can play tricks? SEE!!
So three noses. Three specks of light. And there is a
scream too. Behind me. From way the hell behind me.
And Rivers is saying, close the door. And I'm thinking,
but I don't feel much of a breeze. And she's saying, bolt
it. And she's screaming, get down. GET DOWN!!!
And so I'm down. Why? I didn't ask. Just did it. No
reason. Why the hell argue. But I'll admit to feeling
a touch foolish. When: BANG!!! Then: CRASH!!! The
two sounds as simultaneous as two sounds can be. Can
get. And now I'm covered with glass. A rain of glass, I
think. All fast. One one hundredth of a second, maybe.
That's all. That is it. The time it took. But I felt it all
happen. As in steps. Bang-crash-rain. And I smelled it

too. Get this. Don't forget this. The smell of a sudden, almost immediate, discharge of my SWEAT!!!
And my hair, get this. That was the next thing. The next object of my attention. My hair standing up. But, can you believe this. What I noticed. Not head hair. Not neck hair. But the hair on my knuckles. What an odd sensation. What a strange. The knuckles. Of all places. Of all stupid places. Then. Then I look up. And above me. On the sill tottering. One piece. One small jagged piece of glass. On the edge and tottering. That made me shudder. Really. I want to knock it off. I want to push it back. Anything. Either. It's unnerving. Just as long as it stops tottering on the god damn brink!! I said to myself, something like, "oh no". Not appropriate. Not enough. My hands don't move. Won't budge. Like stumps. Like they had roots. My heart racing. Banging. Like a berserk. Like a berserk something. REACH!? REACH!! DO SOMETHING!! DO SOMETHING!!

(Suddenly, the telephone rings, interrupting the remainder of STUBBS' *entry.)*

*(*STUBBS *and* RIVERS *almost freeze for an instant. Then they turn to* GEORGIA.*)*

(Short pause, as the phone rings.)

GEORGIA: The line was dead just a minute ago.

(Finally. GEORGIA *picks up the phone.* STUBBS *and* RIVERS *watch.)*

GEORGIA: *(Into the phone)* Hello?

RIVERS: *(Quietly. to* STUBBS:*)* Stubbs, do you feel it? The sudden interruption. Everything stops. Then the sense of anticipation. And the mounting tension. Don't you love it?

*(*STUBBS *nods but motions for her to be quiet.)*

GEORGIA: *(To* STUBBS*)* It's them. *(Into the phone)* Yes… Right… I see…. Right… Uh-huh… Uh-huh… Uh-huh… Yes…

RIVERS: *(In a whisper)* There's sort of a built-in suspense 'bout hearing just one side, isn't there? Maybe I should make a note of that. We could use that sometime. What do you think?

*(*STUBBS *nods but again motions for her to be quiet.)*

GEORGIA: *(Into the phone, hiding her face from* STUBBS*)* Yes… Right… I understand…. We won't try to call…. Right… I will…. I said, I will…. I'll tell the Senator….

(Short pause)

*(*GEORGIA *hangs up. Can't look* STUBBS *or* RIVERS*)*

*(*STUBBS*, scared, begins to slowly back up.)*

STUBBS: *(Finally:)* Tell the Senator what? *(No response)* Tell me what?!

RIVERS: *(Looking through her purse)* All I got is maybe. Maybe eighty dollars at best. The rest's in traveler's checks.

STUBBS: Georgia, please.

RIVERS: And Stubbs has. I'll bet he's got less than I do. But if they want it so bad they can have it. *(She reaches for* STUBBS' *wallet.)*

STUBBS: FORGET THE MONEY!!!

(He pushes RIVERS *away, she falls to the floor.)*

STUBBS: *(To* RIVERS*:)* I'm sorry.

GEORGIA: They want you.

STUBBS: They what?

GEORGIA: They said something about an exchange. How you could be real useful to them. But I didn't really understand much of that. *(Short pause. To* RIVERS*)* They don't want us. We'd be let go.

RIVERS: *(Getting up)* Stubbs, I thought it was a robbery.

GEORGIA: They gave you an hour. I guess, 'cause they know we have guns. They said, maybe if we thought about it for a while we wouldn't do anything dumb.

*(*STUBBS *looks down, he fiddles with his watch.)*

GEORGIA: And. And they said one more thing. *(No one looks at her)* They said. They said that killing Winslow. They said that had been a mistake. *(Short pause)* I guess he must have surprised them. Maybe heard them outside or something.

STUBBS: *(Trying to get control of himself, rubs his eyes)* Oh boy.

GEORGIA: What do you think we should do? There's only one neighbor. And they're away for the month. I know, 'cause I'm supposed to be taking in their mail. *(She looks for a response but gets none.)* Except for them, there's nobody within at least a kilometer. *(Short pause)* Did you hear me?

STUBBS: *(Quiet)* What? Just hold it a minute. Just give me a sec to think. Sit down.

(She sits on the bench. Short pause)

GEORGIA: *(Stands)* The milkman's due around six. But that doesn't help, does it?

RIVERS: Sh-sh. Sit down.

(She sits. Short pause)

GEORGIA: *(Stands)* The lecture's in. In less than two hours. Maybe someone'll get concerned enough and drive out here. What do you think?

*(*RIVERS *suddenly and violently grabs* GEORGIA *and throws her back down. She falls over the bench.)*

(For a moment she is dazed, then begins crying.)

GEORGIA: *(Screams:)* WINSLOW, THEY SAID IT WAS A MISTAKE!!!!! *(She cries.)*

(STUBBS suddenly turns to RIVERS and snaps his fingers.)

STUBBS: I'm feeling…I'm feeling angry. Yes! *(He takes a bowl from the table and smashes it on the floor.)*

(GEORGIA shrieks.)

(STUBBS is suddenly calm. He shakes his head. RIVERS crosses out in her notebook what she had just written.)

STUBBS: No. No. That's not what I'm feeling.

(Pause)

(He paces and thinks. GEORGIA confused)

(STUBBS suddenly bellows:)

STUBBS: THOSE PUNKS!! THOSE GOD DAMN PUNKS!!! *(Suddenly calm)* No. No. I don't feel indignant. Not me. *(Pause. He paces.)*

GEORGIA: *(Quietly:)* Rivers…?

STUBBS: I'm feeling…I'm feeling sentimental. Yes!

(Slowly, with tears almost in his eyes, STUBBS approaches RIVERS and tenderly moves his hand across her cheek. Then he looks down, wipes a tear away, reaches up, and rustles her hair. Then suddenly moves away)

STUBBS: No. Not even close. *(Pause. He paces and thinks.)*

GEORGIA: Rivers…?

RIVERS: *(Watching STUBBS)* What?

GEORGIA: What is he doing, Rivers?

RIVERS: *(Notices that STUBBS has stopped pacing)* Sh-sh!

STUBBS: *(Suddenly smiling, arms raised)* I feel happy. I feel full of love! I feel joyous! I do. Yes. I want to wrap my arms around everyone and everything! I do. I do. I

feel majestic. Yes. I feel like I've lived a full life. I feel at
peace with myself. Yes! I feel…. *(Breaks out of it)* Nope.
Nope. I don't feel like that. Nope. Cross it out.

(RIVERS does. Short pause)

GEORGIA: Rivers…?

STUBBS: *(Quickly)* I see my life passing before my eyes!
(Breaks out) Uh-uh. No way. Who am I kidding? *(Paces
and thinks. Short pause)*

GEORGIA: *(Quietly:)* Rivers, do *you* know what he's
doing?

RIVERS: *(Watching STUBBS)* Come again?

GEORGIA: I mean, what he is doing, does it make any
sense to *you*? *(No response: explodes)* DOES IT?!!!!!

STUBBS: *(Suddenly begins backing toward the door)* I'm
alone. And I'm forgotten. I feel small all of a sudden.
Small. And unwanted. And unneeded. I feel like a dark
speck of something against a white space. *(He is against
the door, folding himself, becoming smaller.)* A spec. Just a
faint spec. Getting smaller. Dimmer. Fading fast. Going
out. Being extinguished!! *(Suddenly shouts:)* HELP ME!!!

(GEORGIA is frightened, starts to scream.)

(STUBBS breaks out of it. Calm)

STUBBS: I don't know what to do. There doesn't seem to
be a way out.

(GEORGIA shakes her head and mumbles "no".)

STUBBS: It just don't seem fair. It don't seem to make
any sense. So I'm scared. Yeh.

GEORGIA: No. I don't believe you. No.

(STUBBS sits on the couch.)

GEORGIA: Uh-uh!

RIVERS: Shut up!

GEORGIA: WHY DON'T YOU SHUT UP!!!!!

(Short pause. STUBBS, *looks at both* RIVERS *and* GEORGIA. GEORGIA *walks to the far end of the room, her back to them.)*

STUBBS: *(To* RIVERS:*)* For a second I thought we had something exciting beginning there. But I guess not. Anyway... *(Sits, "begins":)* I find myself on the couch. Maybe what, three, five minutes since the phone call. Since Georgia had said, her voice dull, her voice somber, "You. They want you."

GEORGIA: *(Without looking at him)* Leave me out of this, please.

STUBBS: Since— "They what?" Me. That's me. So, by now, there has been time for it all to sink in. Yes. To soak through. And I feel afraid.

*(*GEORGIA *laughs.)*

STUBBS: I'm scared.

*(*GEORGIA *laughs harder.)*

STUBBS: I don't know where to turn....

*(*GEORGIA *laughs)*

STUBBS: ...or what to do next!!

*(*GEORGIA *laughs very hard.* RIVERS *starts to get up, but* STUBBS *gestures for her to stay back. He goes to* GEORGIA. *She continues to laugh as they look at each other. She stops laughing. Pause. He turns away.)*

STUBBS: Just who the hell am I trying to kid? She's right. *(He walks away.)*

RIVERS: What???

STUBBS: I mean, what a joke. So— "I'm scared". *(He laughs to himself.)* If I'm so scared then just what am I doing worrying about. How I'm going to sound to. Look at us, Rivers. I'm telling you, she's right. I can't really be scared.

RIVERS: Stubbs???

STUBBS: It's all this god damn listening and watching and revealing. That's the. My. I mean, how am I supposed to feel. Even a little scared. If all I do is. I mean, enough is. Jesus Christ, why aren't I doing something. About. Instead of hiding behind some lousy memoir that no one will bother to read anyway. Bother to get to know. Bother to love. And what does this say about. The kind of person I. I don't believe me. I don't. I have taken a very simple idea. A hope. An activity say. And I've gone too. It's sick. Isn't it? Isn't it? How could I not care about. With them out. If not about, then at least about me. I'm human after all, aren't I? AREN'T I?!!!!! (*Short pause. He is almost shaking now. Then to himself:*) Stop it. Stop it, Stubbs. (*Quietly to* RIVERS:) Don't write that down. I'll get better. I'll be better. (*Suddenly turns on* RIVERS:) Will you put that god damn notebook away?!! WILL YOU PUT THAT GOD DAMN NOTEBOOK AWAY?!!!!! (*Pause*) I'll be better. I've got to stop listening to. There's this voice. I can hear it. You can't, I know. It sounds like it's a mile away. I keep wondering, "Mine? Is that mine?" Like in a hollow really. I hear it. Somewhere out there. I mean, in here. It's crying now. It's scared. Afraid. Wailing. And screaming: What are they going to do to me? What are they going to do to me? Help me!! HELP ME!!!!!!! (*He is crying.*)

GEORGIA: He's crying. He's really crying.

(*Pause*)

STUBBS: (*With tears down his face; to* GEORGIA:) Did you like?

(GEORGIA *freezes in shock, staggers a few steps back, looks at* STUBBS, *then* RIVERS. *Suddenly, she runs to the door and begins pounding.*)

GEORGIA: *(Pounding and screaming:)* Help me!!! Help me!!!!

(Blackout)

Scene Four

(Setting: The same)

(Stage dark. Lights fade up.)

(RIVERS sits on the couch, going through her notebook, making corrections, additions, etc. STUBBS stands behind the couch, he pounds its back, thinking.)

(Pause)

(GEORGIA enters with a tray—coffee cups, coffee pot, bottle of milk.)

GEORGIA: I couldn't find the sugar. And I thought it'd just be asking for trouble to turn on the kitchen light to look for it.

(Short pause. GEORGIA sets tray down on the table in front of RIVERS. STUBBS goes to the window and peeks out.)

GEORGIA: I guess I could have pulled the blinds. But I just couldn't face going anywhere near the window. You know what I mean?

RIVERS: *(Without looking up)* What?

(Short pause. STUBBS returns to behind the couch, continues pounding on its back, thinking.)

GEORGIA: *(Pouring herself a cup)* It isn't fresh. I just warmed it up. *(Short pause: no response)* We keep the sugar in the counter cabinet. But, you know, when I felt for it, it wasn't there. *(Pours in some milk, picks up her cup)* I guess, I'll have to ask Winslow where he put it.

(Suddenly, RIVERS looks up at her, and STUBBS turns toward her, both waiting for her reaction. GEORGIA realizes

*what she has just said, freezes for an instant, then drops the
cup, which shatters.)*

(Short pause as GEORGIA *just stares.)*

STUBBS: *(To* RIVERS:) Better. No doubt about it. Much
better than screaming her lungs out. She's catching on.

RIVERS: *(Nods)* Very nice, Georgia.

(STUBBS *returns to his thinking;* RIVERS *to her notebook.*
GEORGIA *sits on the bench and stares.)*

(Pause)

STUBBS: *(Suddenly, without expression)* I feel aggressive.
I've been pushed too far. I've taken just about all I'm
gonna take. I want to fight.

(RIVERS *quickly turns to him. She rifles through the
notebook until she finds the first clean page. She gets set to
write.)*

STUBBS: Where's the rifle?

RIVERS: *(She tries to write this. Stops. Shakes her pen)* Hold
it a second, Stubbs. *(She gets up, goes to her purse.)*

STUBBS: *(At first, not hearing her)* Where's the ri...?!

(Sees RIVERS *is not writing)*

STUBBS: Where are you going? Why aren't you writing?

RIVERS: I'm getting another pen. The other one was
running out.

STUBBS: Wait a minute. Tell me something. And what
am I supposed to do while you're looking for this pen?

RIVERS: It'll just take a second.

STUBBS: How long it'll take doesn't change the fact that
you are holding me up.

RIVERS: I'm sorry, Stubbs.

STUBBS: Sorry for what? Your stupidity? Your incompetence? Your arrogance? Just who the hell do you think you are?

RIVERS: *(Nearly in tears)* It's just that the pen was running...

STUBBS: Look, I don't pay you for excuses. I pay you to write. SO WRITE!!! *(Turns away. Looks around)* NOW, FOR THE LAST TIME, WHERE IS THAT GOD DAMN RIFLE?!!

(RIVERS begins to desperately search her purse.)

RIVERS: *(Without looking up)* It's next to Georgia.

STUBBS: *(Without moving; to GEORGIA)* Give it to me.

(Short pause)

RIVERS: *(Without looking up. To GEORGIA)* Give it to him. *(No response; looks up)* Give it to him!!! ...I'll get it, Stubbs.

STUBBS: No! She is going to have to learn just who is in charge here.... Georgia, the rifle. Hand it to me. That's an order.

(RIVERS continues to dig through her purse.)

(GEORGIA slowly reaches for the rifle, then stops.)

STUBBS: I said, that is an order.

(GEORGIA, very hesitantly, picks up the rifle and hands it to STUBBS.)

(STUBBS suddenly grabs it away from her; he begins to bounce it in his hands, looking it over, nodding and smiling.)

RIVERS: *(In a panic)* Stubbs, I can't find another pen.

STUBBS: *(Explodes:)* GOD DAMN IT, WHAT ARE YOU TRYING TO DO TO ME?!! Do I have to do everything myself? You want a pen? *(Yanks one out of his shirt pocket and flings it across the room.)* There's one.... Now shut up and write!!!!

(RIVERS *chases after the pen, finds it, and hurries to get set to write.* STUBBS *plays with the gun, trying to get back into the "mood".*)

STUBBS: (*"Into" his entry now*) I find a rifle. And for an instant I wait. Expecting. In fact listening for it to somehow bark orders back to me. Into my brain. Back through its barrel. Like Bouganville. With the palm trees. The huts. The steam jackhammers slashing away at the coral. Like my sergeant. Up to his thighs in mud, but still barking. Still in control. Still telling me what to do. Now. Next. Now. (*To rifle:*) SO TELL ME!!!!!!

RIVERS: Stubbs, you won't believe this, but this one doesn't... (*Makes a writing movement*) ...either.

STUBBS: (*Doesn't hear her; to* GEORGIA:) JAM THAT BENCH AGAINST THE DOOR!!! (*Smiles*) I'm surprised by the strength of my voice. The bark of my voice.

(RIVERS *is now up and searching through her coat.*)

GEORGIA: (*Tapping* RIVERS *on the shoulder; trying to remain calm and above it all. She holds the coffee pot.*) Rivers, more coffee?

RIVERS: Leave me alone. Can't you see I'm busy?!!

STUBBS: (*To* GEORGIA:) DO IT!!

GEORGIA: (*Ignoring him, pours herself a cup; to* RIVERS:) Don't hesitate to help yourself, if you change your mind.

STUBBS: (*To himself:*) This the same voice. From the same brain. Which had been. Well, it had been shaking. Almost breaking, in fact. Almost ranting. Maybe this is now just another form of ranting. Maybe. Maybe. This taking charge just another way of giving up on myself. Trying to locate a more comfortable spot somewhere else. Inside someone else. Something else. Maybe. Maybe.

(GEORGIA *suddenly discovers a pencil near the telephone. She waves it at* RIVERS.)

GEORGIA: Rivers, look what I found.

RIVERS: *(To herself as she searches)* I don't believe this. What are the odds against this sort of thing happening?

STUBBS: WHERE IS THAT AMMUNITION BELT?!!!

GEORGIA: *(With pencil)* Rivers. Yoo-hoo. Rivers.

RIVERS: It's just not fair. One pen going dry, maybe. But two!

STUBBS: I find it. I find it myself on the arm of the couch. I throw it over my shoulder. I pat it as if it were alive. *(Pats the ammunition belt)*

GEORGIA: *(With pencil; insistent)* Rivers...!!

RIVERS: Will you get off my back!!!!

STUBBS: *(Yelling at* GEORGIA:*)* I TOLD YOU TO MOVE THAT BENCH!!!!

RIVERS: *(Seeing the pencil; screams:)* WHERE DID YOU GET THAT?!!! *(Grabs the pencil and begins to write)*

STUBBS: *(To himself)* I'm screaming now. That's just what I'm doing. But, shit, maybe I need to scream to shift gears. To move myself onto another thought. Think of what to do next. Now.

(GEORGIA *sits on couch. She tidies up the coffee table, fluffs up the pillows, etc. She ignores* STUBBS *and* RIVERS.)

STUBBS: Look, I'll keep the rifle. Rivers, you take the revolver. And, Georgia, you will be our extra pair of eyes. *(Turns away)* So that is what I'm thinking, is it? Not bad. Not half bad. I had no idea I had such a plan worked out. No idea. Jesus, I wonder what I'm gonna say next.

(GEORGIA *hums quietly to herself.* RIVERS *has picked up the revolver and holds it under her arm as she writes.*)

STUBBS: *(To* RIVERS *and* GEORGIA:*)* We'll stay at the
window. Rivers, you take left. I'll stay right. And
Georgia. Over there. OVER THERE! Get the fuck over
there and keep one eye on the kitchen and scream your
fucking lungs out if you hear so much as a peep. NOW,
DAMN IT! DAMN IT, GET INTO POSITION!!!!

RIVERS: *(To* GEORGIA:*)* YOU HEARD HIM, MOVE IT!!!

*(*GEORGIA *hums and doesn't move.)*

STUBBS: And now I sigh. Now I step back. Step
back and look around. Now I expect to find myself
somehow feeling as if I'd finally climbed into a skin
that will not shudder. Will not shred. But instead.
Yeh. Instead. Get this. I find I can't help smiling at
myself. Can't help wondering if all I am really doing
now is just a fair. Just a decent. Just a pretty good
impersonation. NO! NO!!!

*(*STUBBS *and* RIVERS *at their respective windows.* RIVERS
continues to write.)

STUBBS: So I. Now. As if to try to prove myself wrong.
To prove I have indeed been well cast. That I fit. Fit!
That I belong in this skin. At this time. Under these
conditions. Fit. I WANT TO. I WANT TO FIGHT!!!!
*(He suddenly breaks the window with the butt of his rifle.
Pause.)* But no. Oh shit. No. No. Instead of cementing.
Instead of proving. Get this. The breaking glass only
makes me shudder. Draws me back. And now. Now
even worse I get it into my head. You won't believe
this. I get it into my skull. Where first I'm wondering
if it had really been necessary to break the window. I
think that. Really. I think, how expensive a window is.
Incredible. I don't believe it. How stupid. And now,
second, I begin to see myself as small. As downright
out of place. Out of my element. I begin to feel my
age. And feel awkward. And I begin to see this whole
thing. With the gun. With the window. With the

barking. I begin to see it as a charade. And myself as
embarrassing. As pointless. As sad.

And now I stand. Pull my rifle back. "My" rifle. What
a joke. I stand. Very alone now. Very much alone.
Very red in the face. Very ashamed of myself. WHAT
AM I DOING?!! WHAT THE FUCK AM I DOING
WITH THIS?!!!! *(He throws the rifle down. Covers his face.
Pause. Then, suddenly "out of" the entry, he takes a pack
of cigarettes out of pocket. To* RIVERS:*)* You want one? I
found them in her purse.

*(*RIVERS *nods, finishes her writing.* STUBBS, *breathing
heavily, lights their cigarettes. They smoke.)*

(Short pause)

STUBBS: Good scene.

*(*RIVERS *nods. Pause.)*

*(*GEORGIA *suddenly screams twice.* STUBBS *and* RIVERS *turn
to her.)*

GEORGIA: You know what *I'm* doing? Do you? Huh? I'll
bet you don't. I'll bet you haven't the faintest. Well, am
I right? Or am I right? Well, I'm trying to shake it all
up. All up in here. *(Points to her head)* Figure it couldn't
hurt. No. No. Maybe the pieces will begin to fall into
place. Up here. Couldn't hurt. Couldn't be worse.
Could it? Huh? Huh? *(No response)* DO YOU KNOW
WHAT IT FEELS LIKE?!!! *(To* RIVERS:*)* Do you? To be
standing here. And you. Him. He starts up. He starts
crying. He starts shoutin', do this. Do that. *(To* STUBBS:*)*
And her. She's right with you. The two of you. And
me. I keep thinking. Brother, I sure missed something.
Brother, am I stupid. *(Stops. She screams.)* Nope. Still
doesn't work. Still didn't shake nothin' into place.
But as I was saying. Brother, am I. Am I. What was I
saying. WHAT THE HELL WAS I SAYING?!!!!!

STUBBS: *(Quiet, soothing voice:)* Go on. Go on.

GEORGIA: *(Screams again)* That's better. That's much better. So. Maybe it's because I'm not seeing things so good. What do you think? Possible? Is that possible? Maybe 'cause every time I close my eyes. See, I've closed them. And all I see is: bedroom. Is: blood. So maybe because my mind is. Is what? TELL ME!!! Maybe because of that. You. And her. It all seems so very very odd. Maybe that's why I'm feeling so. Right? Right? Do you think that explains it? Do you? Do you? Please, do you?! TELL ME! TELL ME! PLEASE, SOMEBODY TELL ME! !! *(She covers her face.)*

(Short pause)

(STUBBS applauds, RIVERS join in.)

STUBBS: Bravo. Bravissimo. Bravo.

(GEORGIA looks up, crying.)

GEORGIA: Huh?

STUBBS: *(Walks over to GEORGIA, pats her on the shoulder.)* Georgia. Nice. That was tremendously moving. *(He returns to his thinking.)*

RIVERS: *(Walks over to GEORGIA)* I'm touched. I'm deeply touched.

(RIVERS hugs GEORGIA, turns, returns to her notebook.)

GEORGIA: It...? *(No response)* It was...? *(No response)* It was really good?

(Blackout)

Scene Five

(Setting: The same.)

(Stage dark)

(STUBBS, in black, begins to laugh, almost uncontrollably.)

(Lights up)

(STUBBS *stands center.* GEORGIA *and* RIVERS *are on the couch watching him.* RIVERS *no longer takes notes.*)

STUBBS: *(Continuing with a "story": trying to hold back his laughter, though not succeeding very well)* And so. So for some reason. *(Laughs)* Some God knows why reason, I start to. Because the entire situation here. Them out. Out. This whole fucking picture. *(Laughs, giggles)* With Rivers there concerned. Looking very prim, see. With Georgia almost in. Almost in. In anguish. *(Laughs)* And the window. Let's not forget the window! And with my own face. No doubt. very stiff. Yes. Very serious face. This face. My face. *(Laughs; wipes the tears from his eyes)* So for some reason. It just all becomes hilarious. I don't know why. Just one great big. Big joke, see. That now. That now I'd somehow just been let in on. You see? *(Laughs)* Even though. One side of me. Angry. Yeh. Pissed as hell. Yeh. One side telling me: shut up. SHUT UP! But I can't. I can't. No way. Not for a million bucks. It's too. It's just all too. Why the hell not? It just all too funny now.... *(Laughs out of control. Suddenly stops. Calm. Out of his "story")*

(RIVERS *and* GEORGIA *applaud.*)

(STUBBS *sits on the couch.* RIVERS *stands, thinking, she clears her throat. She takes center stage.*)

(Short pause.)

RIVERS: I'm confused. Or maybe. Better. I'm sort of at odds with myself. On the one hand, see, I want to try to figure out what there is that we *can* do. You know, maybe run for it. It's pretty dark out there. Or go out shooting. I don't know. Whatever. Something like that. But on the other hand, I feel like I should be doing just what I have been doing. Right here with you, Stubbs. Helping you. You know? After all, that is my job, isn't it?

(Short pause)

STUBBS: Start again. More...immediacy, I think. Know what I mean? It sounds like you have it all figured out.

RIVERS: Immediacy. *(Nods)* Okay. *(Clears hers throat. throws back her hair.)* I'm scared. That's here all right. My hands have been shaking so hard it's been difficult to write. Really. I keep hearing those gun shots. And somehow my fingers keep feeling for that revolver. I feel a chill. A chill that's so solid, so physical, it feels like a hit. A punch. A constant banging. Like a heavy cold shower. I can't seem to get comfortable. I want to work. I want to concentrate. After all. After all, that's my job. That's very important to me. But there still is this fear. I guess because of shooting. *Actually* firing. Because I really *did* pull the trigger. I guess 'cause I got started. And then. Then just stopped. Stopped and started waiting. So there's the sense of conclusions, you know, not yet having run their course. Not yet completed their cycle. That sense of an uncompleted motion. A half step. Start-stop. And all too sudden. And the waiting makes it worse. Like the action is still right there, I just gotta grab it. The action is just waiting for me to finish it. So the sense of being pulled at. Tugged at. This way. And that. Well, it sometimes has even felt like I was splitting apart. Like, see, I'm breaking in half. Then. Then it's real bad. What I'm feeling. Then, it's terrible. Then it's real bad. What I'm feeling. Then, it's terrible. It's a nightmare. Then: Jesus. JESUS CHRIST. STUBBS, IT'S SO GOD DAMN AWFUL, I CAN'T STAND IT!!!! *(Breaks down. Short pause. It takes her a little while to get calm.)*

(Applause)

(RIVERS *returns to the couch.)*

STUBBS: *(Takes* RIVERS' *hand and winks)* Better. Much better.

(She sits.)

(GEORGIA *stands, nervous.*)

GEORGIA: Well, I guess I feel, you know. Well, sort of privileged. In a way. After all, you're a Senator and I'm. Well, who the hell am *I*, you know?

(STUBBS *has been listening intently; snaps his fingers:* GEORGIA *stops; he goes to* GEORGIA, *almost whispers to her:*)

STUBBS: Look, Georgia. It is always obvious when one is faking the emotion. Do you understand? And when it is obvious, there is no interest. When there's no interest, no point. No point, then why do it? You understand?

(*She nods.* STUBBS *returns to the couch.*)

GEORGIA: I am feeling…. (*Short pause*) I guess I'm feeling, you know…resentful.

(*She looks for a reaction,* STUBBS *nods.*)

GEORGIA: I mean, well. You come into here. My house. This *is* my house. Where *I* live. And. And mostly you. But also her. You come into here and you keep doing this stuff. And I'm made to feel like I'm the one who is intruding. That I'm the one butting in. That I don't belong here.
And then. When we realize what's happened. When I'm frightened. When I keep thinking and I can't get it out of my mind, and I feel guilty even trying. Thinking that Winslow is dead. When, as you know too. When what happened to Winslow will probably happen to us, too. That all this isn't over. Not by any means. Not by a long shot. When all this has happened in my house. And in my head. And I turn and look for what? Maybe just a little tiny bit of concern. Of consolation. Not only because of Winslow. But also because we're all in this together. Stuck together, almost. No choice. Well, there should be, I keep telling myself.

There should be some mutual concern. A certain togetherness. A "let's help each other" spirit. But you. You not only don't put your arm around me. Give me a shoulder to... But you make me feel like I'm fucking butting in. Like I should go away. Well, where should I go? WHERE THE HELL SHOULD I GO?!!!!!!

I don't know. See. It's all become like a dream. That I can't remember anymore. Nothing specific. Just this feeling. This aftertaste. But still. But I know it's still not over. So I keep pricking myself. Keep thinking, you are not really there. No. 'Cause if you were. If you were there, I wouldn't be feeling so much hate and disgust for you. So much resentment. I wouldn't be feeling like, even though I'm in my own god damn house, I'm stuck somewhere else. Some place I've never been before. Somewhere. Where I'm all alone.

(Short pause. GEORGIA, close to tears, closes her eyes, not knowing what to expect.)

(STUBBS claps loudly. RIVERS applauds and whistles.)

(GEORGIA opens her eyes and smiles, pleased.)

(The applause stops. GEORGIA sits, STUBBS stands, thinking.)

(Pause)

GEORGIA: Can I try one more?

(Blackout)

Scene Six

(Setting: The same.)

(Stage dark. Lights fade up.)

(STUBBS, GEORGIA, and RIVERS are waiting. Each is doing something idiosyncratic, like clicking their nails, jiggling a

foot, etc. GEORGIA *also reads a book.* STUBBS *and* RIVERS *on the couch.* GEORGIA *is on the bench.)*

(Pause)

(Gun shot, off. The vase on the table explodes.)

(They are startled, jump.)

*(*GEORGIA *stands slowly. She drops her book. The others watch her. She does not look down. She fiddles with her bracelet. No expression on her face. Her hands shake.)*

GEORGIA: *(Finally:)* I keep seeing his face. I keep seeing Winslow's face up there. *(She starts to cry. She begins to take a step toward center but stops, covers her face, lowers her head, then raises her head slowly and suddenly screams.)*

STUBBS: *(Stands; angry:)* Oh fuck, I'm getting real tired of this. SHUT UP!!!

RIVERS: *(Holding him back)* Stubbs, she's upset.

STUBBS: Oh she is, is she. Well what do you think I am, huh? I'm upset too. ME TOO!! But least I make the effort to control myself. Make the effort to keep a lid on this. Keep myself together. LEAST I'M NOT SCREAMING EVERYONE'S BRAINS LOOSE!!

*(*GEORGIA *screams.)*

STUBBS: I SAID, STOP THAT!!

(He grabs at GEORGIA's *arm. She turns toward him and spits in his face.* STUBBS *is taken aback but very angry now. He wants to hit her.* RIVERS *jumps up and grabs* STUBBS.)*

RIVERS: Don't touch her, Stubbs! *(She pushes him away. To* GEORGIA*)* You shouldn't have done that, Georgia. *(Puts her arm around* GEORGIA*)* Hey, take it easy. Come on. Come on. It's all forgotten. There. There.

(Comforts her. GEORGIA *starts sobbing. Short pause)*

(Suddenly, everyone calm, they all nod at each other and return to their earlier positions. STUBBS *and* RIVERS *on the couch, etc.)*

(Pause)

(EXPLOSION off. Every one turns to the door. RIVERS *gets up and peeks out the window.)*

RIVERS: *(To* STUBBS;*)* Georgia's car's on fire.

GEORGIA: *("In shock")* What?! *My* car?!! *(She gets up and charges toward the window.)*

RIVERS: *(Trying to stop her)* Don't get too close.

*(*GEORGIA *fights to get away.)*

RIVERS: I said, don't get too close! Stop kicking!

*(*GEORGIA *bites her hand.)*

RIVERS: She bit me!! She bit me!!

*(*RIVERS *slaps her across the face,* GEORGIA *falls to the floor.* RIVERS *walks away, rubbing her hand.)*

STUBBS: *(To* RIVERS;*)* Let me see. *(Looks at her hand)* You'll live. *(Smacks her on the fanny. He goes over to* GEORGIA.*)* Georgia…

GEORGIA: *(Pointing toward the door)* But *my*…!

RIVERS: *(Rubbing her hand)* She broke the skin.

STUBBS: *(Giving* GEORGIA *his hand)* I know. I know.

(She takes it. He pulls her up. Short pause. They all "break", become calm, nod, pleased with each other, and return to their former positions. Pause)

GEORGIA: *(She starts to wipe her hands on her dress, then notices the blood. She tenses and mumbles:)* Those bastards.

STUBBS: What did you say, Georgia?

GEORGIA: Never mind.

STUBBS: Georgia, if you have something to say, you should say it.

RIVERS: Stubbs is right. Get it off your chest, Georgia. You'll feel better.

GEORGIA: *(Holding up part of her bloody dress)* I said, "Those bastards".

STUBBS: And how do you feel about those bastards? Do you hate them?

(GEORGIA nods)

STUBBS: Then say it like you do.

GEORGIA: *(With hate)* Those bastards!

STUBBS: You want to strangle them with your own hands, don't you?

GEORGIA: *(Nods; with more anger:)* Those bastards!!!

STUBBS: You want to tear their eyes out!

GEORGIA: *(Standing, yelling)* THOSE BASTARDS!!!!

STUBBS: That's it!

GEORGIA: *(She grabs a pillow from the couch and begins punching it and shouting:)* THOSE BASTARDS! THOSE BASTARDS!

STUBBS: THAT'S IT!! THAT'S IT!!

GEORGIA: *(Screams:)* THOSE GOD DAMN BASTARDS!!!!

(Short pause. They all "break", become calm, and return to their former positions. Pause.)

RIVERS: *(Finally:)* It's still your turn, Stubbs.

STUBBS: *(Suddenly angry)* DON'T YOU THINK I KNOW THAT!!! *(Calm:)* That felt nice.

(Pause)

GEORGIA: Did I tell you about what I was feeling in the car? When I was driving you two here?

STUBBS: *(To* RIVERS*:)* Did she?

*(*RIVERS *nods.)*

GEORGIA: Oh.

(Pause)

STUBBS: I feel nothing. Nothing. Not a thing. As if my emotions, so stretched. So strained. Have not bent, but broken. And so now, like maybe snapped ends of a wire, they lay limp. Unable to make any connection. ... That's a possibility. *(He thinks.)*

(Pause)

GEORGIA: Did I tell you about how I felt at your hotel? My frustration? My confusion? My pent-up anger?

STUBBS: Did she?

RIVERS: Yes.

GEORGIA: Oh.

(Pause)

STUBBS: I feel...everything. All at once. A mess and a blur of feelings. Wires crossed... That's also a possibility. *(He thinks.)*

(Pause)

GEORGIA: Did I tell you about how I was feeling when those men out there called?

*(*STUBBS *turns to* RIVERS *as if to say "Did she?"* RIVERS *nods.)*

GEORGIA: Oh.

(Pause)

GEORGIA: Did I tell you about how I felt when I found Winslow?

STUBBS: Did she?

RIVERS: No.

(GEORGIA *slaps her hands together and takes center stage.*
STUBBS *and* RIVERS *watch.*)

GEORGIA: Well. Well, see, I guess you could say I was
already worried. See, I hadn't admitted it to myself,
you know. The kind of worry that you only feel but
don't allow yourself to think. I mean, after he wasn't
in the kitchen. After I'd seen the roast still in the sink.
I felt, well, I guess I even thought—"heart attack". I
think I even said to myself: "heart attack". So, see, I
was already pretty anxious when I started up the steps
to the bedroom. I was already holding my breath and
jumping for explanations. I was already seeing, you
know, expecting to see a note on our bureau telling me
he'd got a call from the office. And I was already angry
at him for leaving and forgetting about the roast.
So, when I tried to open the door, and it was jammed.
Not locked. But jammed so I could only open it a
couple of inches. I had no thought. Nothing. This just
didn't fit. What the hell could this have to do with
that note on our bureau I kept "seeing". So I pushed.
With all my strength. I pressed my shoulder against
and pushed. And then. And then—a foot. Only a foot.
PUSH! PUSH, GEORGIA! HEART ATTACK!! PUSH!!
Then—blood. Then as the door inched open. Then—

(*Suddenly,gun shots rip a line of holes across the door.*)

(*Everyone turns to the door.*)

(GEORGIA *steps upstage.*)

STUBBS: (*Quietly*) Here they come.

RIVERS: It won't be long now.

GEORGIA: I guess not.

STUBBS: *(Taking center stage)* Now, let me think—my last words. I am going to need some appropriate last words. *(He thinks. Short pause)*

RIVERS: Now that you mention it, Stubbs, I guess, so will I. *(She takes center. Short pause)*

GEORGIA: Me too. *(Takes center. Short pause)*

RIVERS: What about...? No. No.

(Short pause)

STUBBS: I've got mine.... No. No.

(Short pause)

GEORGIA: How does this sound.... Nah.

(Short pause)

RIVERS: Uh. No. Too maudlin.

(Short pause)

STUBBS: Yeh. Too clever.

(Short pause)

GEORGIA: I have mine! Wait. I just lost it.... Shit, it's right on the tip of my tongue....

(Short pause)

(Gun shot blast—the door is shot off its hinges and crashes to the floor.)

(They all turn and look.)

(Blackout)

Scene Seven

(Setting: Vienna. Sitting room of a hotel suite. Same as Scene One.)

(Two years later)

(Stage dark. Lights up)

(RIVERS *sits on the chaise.* GUNTER *stands center.)*

GUNTER: It was a winter's evening, two years ago
today, when a black American limousine sped through
the narrow side streets of Vienna. In the back seat, the
American senator thumbed through an issue of *The
Herald Tribune.* He read the football scores first. And
then the news. As he pressed his face to the window,
he saw a cathedral. He noticed that the breath of the
pedestrians created small clouds in the air. As they
passed a Coca Cola sign, he smiled to himself. The
senator sat back as the car lurched forward, headed for
an intimate Viennese hotel. This hotel. Where upstairs,
in Suite 812, a bald-headed man paced his room,
avoiding every squeak in the floor.
Suddenly, this man stops and pulls back the lace
window curtain. He looks down on the street below.
He keeps the light off and one hand over part of his
face. He turns the yellow knob of the radio and listens
to a Strauss waltz. He smokes American cigarette after
American cigarette. He waits.
The limousine glides up in front of the green awning of
the hotel. I hurry outside and bow as a porter is trained
to bow. That is, without much to do. The senator
grips my shoulder and winks. The elevator jerks and
squeaks, but the senator calls the ride smooth. His
bags are of the softest leather. Other guests on the
same floor have left their doors open just a crack. They
wish to get a peek of the famous American senator. An
inconspicuous peek.
One door, however, remains closed. The door to Suite
812. Where, inside, the bald headed man is practicing
putting a drinking glass against a connecting door. The
one which connects his room with Suite 814.
A couple of guests now find excuses to wander the
hall. One says she is looking for her shoes. The senator
slaps everyone on the back. He shakes two different

hands at the same time. He retires to his suite. Number
814.

I return to the lobby. I find myself humming.
Something by Liszt. I catch my reflection in a mirror
which has a pattern in gold leaf. I wink at myself. I
practice shaking two hands at the same time. I whistle
"O Susannah".

But upstairs. The man in 812 has grabbed for a phone.
He is dialing. The call is answered on the first ring.
"The country!" He wants to scream, but forces out
a whisper. "Yes, the country. Senator Stubbs will be
having dinner in the country." And he hangs up. He
lights the last of his American cigarettes. He pats the
spot on his chest, making sure the bulge made of metal
is still there. Weeks later, it would be learned that this
man had been trained in the Middle East. That he was
an expert with explosives. That his father was a retired
schoolteacher from Burgenland. That his aunt writes
poetry. And that his mother had died when he was
twelve.

And so the course of events, which were soon to
be played out in a farmhouse. With terrorists. With
death. With fear. That course of events which would
dominate the headlines and gossip of Vienna for
weeks. Had been set in motion. It had begun. It had
begun here. In this hotel. Right here! In suite 812. And
in suite 814. Just two years ago today.

(Short pause. GUNTER *looks for a response.)*

RIVERS: *(Nods:)* Thank you, Gunter. Very charming. I
will have the senator call you when he wakes up.

(Short pause. GUNTER *doesn't move.)*

RIVERS: Is there something else, Gunter?

*(*GUNTER *gestures with his head toward the pile of books on
the desk.)*

RIVERS: Oh, of course! Of course, the book. How stupid of me to forget. By all means, Gunter, take a copy of the senator's memoirs. I'm sure he'd want you to have one. The top copy, yes. I believe that one is already signed.

(GUNTER *takes a copy and checks to see if it is signed.*)

RIVERS: And thank you again, Gunter, for that very lovely story. The senator will be thrilled to learn that he has become part of the history of this hotel.

(GUNTER *exits with book.*)

(STUBBS *enters from the bedroom. His hair disheveled; he wears a smoking jacket; he holds a large new book—his published memoirs.*)

RIVERS: Stubbs, don't you think Gunter is cute?

STUBBS: Who?

RIVERS: Gunter. The porter. He just told me the cutest little story.

STUBBS: Forget Gunter and tell me what you think about the election night story.

RIVERS: About the what?

STUBBS: I'm thinking of giving it for the lecture tonight. You think there'd be interest in that kind of thing?

RIVERS: The election night story? But I thought you were going to do our rescue story. I even think that's what they're counting on, Stubbs.

STUBBS: Forget that. And just tell me if you think they'll go for this. (*Opens the book*)

RIVERS: But, Stubbs, they have even named the lecture series after Georgia. You know, as sort of a memorial. Wait a minute, I think I've got the flyer here somewhere.

STUBBS: Look. I know what happened. You know what happened. They know what happened. I'm tired of

that story. You're tired of that story, and, damn it, I'll
bet they're just as tired of it too. So let's just forget it,
okay?

RIVERS: Tired of it? What with us having given
up hope. What with guns blazing. And bullets
everywhere. And fire and smoke so you couldn't see
you hand in front of your face. What with the two of us
behind the couch. You patting my head. And me. I'm
shaking like a. And Georgia! Georgia! Where the hell is
she?! Georgia! We're screaming. We're choking. When
suddenly, outside, we begin to hear…

STUBBS: *(Cuts her off)* Rivers, come on, I'm sick of telling
it, okay? Come on and listen to this.

RIVERS: Sure, Stubbs. If that's what you want.

STUBBS: Well, that is what I want. Now just tell me
whether you think they're gonna go for this. …Where
the hell are my glasses.

RIVERS: I'll check the bedrooms. *(Gets up)*

STUBBS: No. Why the hell don't you read it. That might
be interesting. Maybe I can hear it better that way and
be able to tell myself whether it'll play or not. Here.
(Hands her the book) Where it's marked.

RIVERS: "Election night. I was in my suite"?

STUBBS: That's it. I'll stand back here. So it's more like
it'll be. You ready?

(RIVERS nods.)

STUBBS: Then, let's hear it. And for God's sake take
your time. This ain't a race, okay?

RIVERS: Okay. *(Short pause; she clears her throat; reads:)*
"Election night. I was in my suite at the Hotel Pierre.
Three televisions were set in front of me. One for each
network. I lounged with my shoes off on the couch.
Friends, supporters, news people made a steady

stream past me. I felt like I was holding some sort of
court. I remember laughing to myself at the thought. I
stretched my legs out but just couldn't get comfortable.
I tried to eat, but my stomach already felt full. That's
how tense I was. Trying to relax, I took a shower. But
still felt dirty. I felt like I smelled as soon as I toweled
myself off. I put my shoes back on so I'd feel like I
didn't have to relax. That I wouldn't feel pressured to
relax.

"The first returns had come hours before. A small town
in Vermont. I won the town by twenty-three votes.
And made a joke about it. Something like, "Now we
just gotta run even." Everyone laughed. Real hard.

"As the East Coast states started to come in. I surprised
everyone by going to bed. I'm playing this cool, I
thought. I wondered if I'd wake up the President. Or
a loser. When I did wake up, I thought I'd been asleep
for hours, but it'd been only seconds. My sense of time
was all warped. I felt a little bit foolish when I returned
to the televisions so soon. But we all just laughed about
it. Real hard.

"As the network projections were being flashed state
by state, I got into the differing graphics of the three
stations. One gave the percentage inside an American
flag. Another within a group of stars. And the third
had the map of the state that was in question. I thought
about what I'd have chosen if the graphics were my
job. I didn't come up with much.

"By midnight we were neck and neck. It was becoming
obvious that California would be the big casino. One
roll. One very big roll of the dice. It'd come down to
that. I tried to name all the cities in California that I'd
visited. I gave up after thirty. That's enough, I thought.
You should have no regrets. So we all relaxed because
we knew California wouldn't be final for a couple of
hours. We all breathed easy. Getting ourselves set to

start that slow move to the edge of our chairs as the minutes began to tick away. For the first time that night, I took a drink. I told myself I'd just sip it slowly. Make it last until California.

"But then. I never even had the chance to take a drop. Because. Because suddenly it was flashed! Ohio had changed hands! We'd lost it! We'd won it and now we'd lost it! There'd been a mistake. A big mistake. It was suddenly. What happened? WHAT HAPPENED?!! IT WAS OVER! IT WAS OVER! California wasn't enough. WE NEEDED OHIO!!!!!! *(Short pause. She is very "into" the story. Almost has to fight back tears)*

"I couldn't think of anything to do. I couldn't think of anything I wanted to do. Except *not* cry. Not cry like *they* were. Like everyone around me was. My actions, then, they became *not* actions. Do you see what I mean? I was *not* going to give up. I was *not* going to bed. I was *not* going to break down. I was *not* going to win". *(She shuts the book; takes a handkerchief and wipes her eyes. Pause)*

STUBBS: *(Half-smile)* I. I really do feel for that man. And so will they. It will play. It will play. It will play.

(Blackout)

END OF PLAY